PRAISE FOR *WISHWORK*

"Write your wish. See your wish. Live your wish. Alexa helps you turn a general inkling into a specific manifestation. Go make your ruckus."

—Seth Godin, author of *The Dip*

"Reading Wishwork *is spending a delightful few hours enjoying Alexa's sorely-needed optimism. Alexa takes the reader on the journey from merely making a wish to turning the wish into a daily motivating force. She leaves no doubt we are the architects of our dreams."*

—Ellen Lubin-Sherman, author and speaker

"Alexa takes something that we all did as kids—tossing pennies into the fountain and forgetting all about them until our birthday when we blow out the candles—and makes it feel delightful and practical. This book is a ray of sunshine and the perfect reminder that yes, wishes really do come true—when you do the work. And the Wishwork doesn't feel like work at all."

—Jacq Fisch, unfussy writer, editor, and writing coach

"So much of our success depends on our beliefs, our focus, and our vision for the future. Wishbeads is the belief, the focus, and the vision incarnate—right there on your wrist. The fact that we can wear these gentle reminders in an of-the-moment bracelet stack is a bonus for those of us who want to wear our promise of tomorrow with style. Wishwork shows us the path to bring those intentions to life."

—Julie Cantor, MD, JD attorney, academic, and founder and CEO of Harlen

"No one who has met Alexa can doubt her gift for transforming people with her special blend of earthly and otherworldly wisdom. Here, she engages her whole spirit in the task of helping make people's dreams come true, no less—translating lofty mystical ideas into joyfully approachable action steps that have the surest chance of yielding results. Alexa herself is living proof that the simple yet profound act of wishing, not only with sincerity but also with structure, can produce an outstandingly blessed life."

—Shani Raja, former *Wall Street Journal* editor

"Alexa's brilliant Wishwork process provides a practical, tangible blueprint for making us all a little bit happier and the world a little bit brighter. This book will inspire you, challenge you, and give you hope that anything is possible. Make a wish and come along for the journey—you won't be disappointed!"

—Anna Robertson, VP of Growth & Partnerships, ABC

"After joyfully receiving my first Wishbeads as a gift, during a transitional period in my life, I decided to pass on the magic to several close friends. Without exception, each one said some version of, 'This is so perfect for me right now! How did you know?' Often, with tears in their eyes. With Wishwork, Alexa beautifully reconnects us to our personal power and shows us the path to our best and brightest life. Together, they are magical."

—Courtney Thorne-Smith, Actress

WISHWORK

WISHWORK

Make a Wish, Do the Work, and Watch It Come True

ALEXA FISCHER

The Tiny Press

CORAL GABLES

For permission requests, please contact the publisher at:

The Tiny Press
Mango Publishing Group
2850 Douglas Road, 2nd Floor
Coral Gables, FL 33134 USA
info@mango.bz

For special orders, quantity sales, course adoptions and corporate sales, please email the publisher at sales@mango.bz. For trade and wholesale sales, please contact Ingram Publisher Services at customer.service@ingramcontent.com or +1.800.509.4887.

Library of Congress Cataloging
ISBN: (print) 978-1-64250-023-3 (ebook) 978-1-64250-024-0

Library of Congress Control Number: 2018964362
BISAC category code: SEL004000—SELF-HELP / Affirmations

Printed in the United States of America

This book is dedicated to anyone with a small wish, a big wish, a secret wish, a public wish, any type of wish that you want to bring into reality.

If you don't have a clear wish yet, but you'd like to make one, this book is for you, too.

And if you've been discouraged many times in the past, if you've disappointed other people (or yourself), if you feel hesitant to open your heart and start dreaming and wishing again, you, *especially* you...this book is dedicated to *you*.

TABLE OF CONTENTS

WATCH IT COME TRUE

FINAL THOUGHTS

FOREWORD

Have you ever met someone who can walk into any room and, as soon as they arrive, the energy in the room is just...different? They walk in and *Kapow!* Things feel brighter, sparklier, almost like someone flipped a light switch.

Alexa Fischer is one of those people.

When Alexa decided to attend one of my writing retreats in Hawaii, I was thrilled. We'd met once before and I knew she'd be a wonderful addition to the group.

She told me, "A lot has changed since the last time we saw each other. I've started a new company called Wishbeads." Then she asked, "Is it OK if I bring some Wishbeads products along to the retreat?"

Without really knowing what a "Wishbead" was, I said, "Of course!" because I figured anything from Alexa's mind and heart would be delightful.

On the final night of the retreat, after five beautiful days of writing, hiking, yoga, and inspiring conversations, Alexa did a Wishbeads presentation. We sat around a big table snacking on chocolate after dinner, and Alexa invited everyone to close their eyes. She asked us to imagine a bright light beaming from our hearts, beaming out, out, out, and creating a big canvas—almost like a projector or a movie screen. She asked us to sit quietly, watching, allowing images to unfold on that screen.

"On that screen, you will see your greatest wish," she said.

(If you're a cynical New Yorker, at this point you might be thinking, *Uh, this is some hippie-dippie nonsense…*and if you're from Los Angeles you might be thinking, *Oh yes, I do this all the time at my Thursday night visionary chakra cleansing seminar! So fun!* As for me, I tend to fall somewhere in the middle. I like mystical, spiritual explorations and I like practical action steps and Excel spreadsheets, too.)

So there I was, eyes closed, with my imaginary movie screen, waiting for my "greatest wish" to appear. At first I saw nothing. I felt a little worried. Then my mind started bopping around to wishes that I thought I ought to have—like having a bestselling book, or being on national TV, or having two hundred and fifty thousand dollars in my savings account. But as I allowed myself to relax and breathe, something unexpected happened.

I saw my wish on the screen—and it wasn't what I expected to see.

It was a sweet, simple moment. Winter time. Snow falling outside. I was snuggled in bed. A fireplace crackled nearby. Candles flickered. I felt so incredibly peaceful. On the wall there was a calendar—one of those big calendars that's about a foot and a half wide. On the calendar was…nothing. No appointments. No obligations. No pressures. A completely blank slate. I felt this incredible feeling of freedom and spontaneity—like I could pack a bag, hop on a plane, and go visit my family (they live in another state) and there was nothing to stop me from going. I had all the time and space in the world.

I felt my eyes welling up with tears and I knew, *Right now, this is my greatest wish. I wish for more quiet time, more free time, more time to relax and make memories with the people I love.*

A few moments later, Alexa invited us to write down our greatest wish on a piece of paper and then roll it up into a little cylinder.

Then, she showed us how to glue and snip those cylinders of paper into a collection of beads—beads that could be worn as a bracelet.

"Now you can wear your wish right on your wrist," she explained.

That day in Hawaii, Alexa invited me to see my wish clearly, write it down, and wear it. But of course, as we all know, it's not enough to just write something down and look at it and think about it. We need to *act* on it, too. That's exactly what Alexa illustrates so beautifully inside this book—how to take concrete, actionable steps every day, propelling yourself closer and closer to your ultimate wish.

Alexa is truly a masterful Wisher. She has wished for so many things—like a chance to meet with Oprah's magazine team, a fluffy white rescue dog and a red Shasta RV trailer. Whatever she wishes for, she always finds a way to make it come true— getting exactly what she envisioned, or something very close! She has survived many hardships—dealing with rejection (so many auditions!) and frustrations as an actress, and dealing with frightening health challenges in her family—and yet her outlook on life is relentlessly optimistic.

I can't imagine a better person to write a book like this one—a book about how to make your own wishes come true. No fairy godmother or magic genie required. Just your own mind, heart, capable hands, and a willingness to put in some effort.

Whatever you're wishing for, I'm excited for your journey with Alexa to begin...

Alexandra Franzen
April 16, 2018—Portland, Oregon

Let's Get Started

HELLO, WISHER!

Hello, brave and beautiful Wisher! This is Alexa. No, I'm not the Echo Dot robot from Amazon.com. I'm an actual human being. I live in Santa Monica, California, with my husband, two kids, and a fluffy rescue dog that I wished for (...and then he showed up in my life because wishes really do come true!) but that's a story for another time.

For most of my life, I've worked as an actress. You may have seen me in TV shows like *NCIS*, *Bones*, *Lie To Me* and dozens of commercials. For many years, I've also worked as a communication and public speaking trainer, which means I coach people who are getting ready for important moments like job interviews, presentations, media appearances, or even first dates! I love helping people feel more confident and shine brightly as they move through the world.

But then, a few years ago, I launched myself into a completely new line of work: creating a jewelry company called Wishbeads.

I had zero experience crafting or making jewelry (seriously, none). And I had zero experience in product manufacturing, shipping, distribution, and all the logistical left-brain stuff that's required to run this type of business. But I felt strongly compelled to make Wishbeads happen, so I started researching, taking baby steps, and figuring out how to do it. It was an exciting and challenging process filled with so many *"Ack, but I don't know what to dooooo!"* moments. But I kept going. And I'm still going. Wishbeads is growing with each passing year. (I'll share a little more about my "building a business" story in a few pages.)

Why am I telling you all of this? Firstly, because I'll be your guide throughout this book so I figure I ought to introduce myself. Secondly, because I want you to know that I understand how it feels to have a big, daunting wish. A wish that feels exciting and, frankly, overwhelming. I know how it feels to stare at your computer and wonder, *How the heck am I going to pull this off?* and *Can I really achieve this, or am I delusional?* and *Will this crazy idea even work?* I know those feelings because I've felt—and still feel—those doubts all the time.

It's normal to feel doubts as you move through your life—everyone does, hey, we're only human!—however, you don't have to let those doubts stop you from pursuing your dreams.

I sincerely hope you won't let that happen.

I hope this book gives you that little extra nudge of support, positivity, optimism, and encouragement that you need to make your greatest wishes come true.

Please don't give up.

I believe in me...and I believe in you.

Wishes really can, and do, come true.

What Is a Wish?

The dictionary defines the word "wish" as "a desire or hope for something to happen." Similar words include: "longing, yearning, inclination, urge, craving, hunger."

Sometimes, in our society, wishing gets a bad reputation. It's considered frivolous or foolish. When you accuse someone of "wishful thinking," it's not much of a compliment! You're basically saying, "Get real. You're being delusional."

But I don't think wishing is delusional. I believe that wishing is very powerful. When you make a wish, you're connecting with what you really want. You're saying, "This matters to me." You're saying, "I'm ready to focus, put in some work, and transform my life so that I can have what I want."

Wishing is not merely the stuff of child's play—like tossing pennies into fountains or puffing out birthday candles after a celebratory song. Wishing is all about moving closer to the life you truly desire—your best possible life. That's not foolish. That's fantastic!

A New Way to Wish

Perhaps you've made a lot of wishes in the past, but they haven't always come true. Perhaps, after experiencing a string of disappointments, you've decided, "Wishing is pointless. It never works."

Rather than deciding, "Oh, wishing is dumb and it never leads anywhere," let's try a new perspective. It's time to start wishing in a new way. It's time for a different (and more effective) approach!

Successful wishing starts with how you feel—your mood, your emotions, your attitude about the world. Some people refer to these feelings as your "vibration" or your "energy." Let me break it down for you...

Your energy determines how your day is going to unfold.

If you're feeling anxious, the world seems like one giant hazard zone.

If you're feeling grateful, you see abundance at every turn.

If you're feeling angry, every human being appears to be against you.

If you're feeling loving, others tend to love you right back.

Whatever you're focusing on, that's what you're bringing into your awareness and into your experience. Your energy is creating your life. And your energy is shaping the world.

"Give me a break, Alexa. Am I creating global warming? The swings of the stock market? Social inequality? Am I creating all that?!" you might wonder.

Maybe not completely. But on some level, yes, you are. Every human being is, in some way or another, creating and shaping the world that we live in.

No, I don't think you're responsible for the ice caps melting per se, but you are responsible for how you feel and what you choose to do with your feelings. Your feelings are going to determine your actions, and your actions are going to determine a great deal of what happens in your individual life and in the rest of the world, too.

For example, let's say you're feeling exasperated and deflated about the massive island of plastic floating in the middle of ocean poisoning all the fish, but then you habitually use a plastic straw at every restaurant—never considering where it ends up—simply because you feel overwhelmed and powerless. You feel like the problem is so darn huge, so what could you possible do about it? *Sigh*...sip, sip, sip.

On the other hand, perhaps you look around and see the pain and suffering of the growing number of people who have found themselves homeless. However, you might choose to feel overwhelmed and powerless and do nothing to help. Or you could make a different choice. You could choose to feel empathetic, curious, and excited to find solutions. You could choose to ask yourself, *What can I do about this?* That's exactly what two amazing women—Steph Johnson and Nina Leilani Deering—chose to do. These women co-founded Voices of Our City, a weekly choir that meets in a church in downtown San Diego. The chorus is comprised of some fine folks who are sleeping on the streets and gather to sing their hearts out every Friday at noon. This choir has given dozens of homeless men and women a safe space to connect, make art, express themselves, and be perceived by the community in a new light. So beautiful! A creative solution that has led to advocacy, awareness, hope, and transformation.

Two dire situations. Two different responses. Two different outcomes.

To connect all of this back to wishing...

Often, the only difference between a wish that comes true and a wish that *doesn't* is how you choose to feel about the situation.

Will you choose to feel overwhelmed and powerless? Or will you choose to feel curious, optimistic, and hopeful? Your feelings determine your actions, and your actions determine your results.

HOW WISHING WORKS

When you know what you want, it's a heck of a lot easier to go and get it, right?

Let's say you're hungry. You've got that gnawing sensation in your stomach and, though you have no intention of cooking, all you can think about is enjoying a delicious meal.

You then head out to a local restaurant, grab a seat and wait for the waiter to arrive.

When he does, he smiles at you, pen and paper at the ready, and asks, "What can I get for you today?"

"Food," you manage to blurt out because you're too hungry to think straight.

So the waiter says, "What are you in the mood for?"

Your eyes get big, imagining the taste of various cuisines. Instantly you remember, "Italian! I love Italian."

"Great...sounds good," he continues, "are you in the mood for pasta?"

"Yes, pasta!" Your mouth is watering now.

"Wonderful, we have spaghetti, linguini, penne, ravioli, and farfalle."

You mind races at all these possible options and then WHAM— you remember how much you love ravioli.

"Ravioli, please."

"Sounds great. Would you like spinach and ricotta ravioli with cream sauce or butternut squash ravioli in a light brown butter sage sauce?"

"Oh, the butternut squash ravioli, please." You can practically taste it as the words roll off your tongue. A short while later, you are in pasta heaven. Perfection! Big grin, happy belly.

Let's break this scenario down.

At first, you know you're starving, but you don't know what you want. If you simply told the waiter that you wanted food, without any additional details, you may or may not have been pleased with what he served you. Without being told—or given any hint whatsoever—chances are you would have been given a dish that would have satisfied your hunger, but not necessarily thrilled or delighted you.

A hamburger can be ho-hum if you really wanted Italian instead! And it's not just any type of Italian food, it was a specific dish that tickled your fancy. Oh, that butter sage sauce! *Delicious.*

Now imagine that the "Universe" is the waiter.

(Please note: The "Universe" that I am referring to can be called many things, but I like to think of it as divine energy or source energy—the place from which we all came from and where we will likely return. I welcome you to substitute whatever language feels most appropriate to you, like God, Goddess, Love, or whatever term feels right.)

So, the idea here is that the Universe wants to bring you whatever your heart desires. It's there, every moment of every day, listening for the details of exactly what you want—listening for the things that will make your heart sing and your soul be satisfied. Listening with a pen and paper in hand, ready to jot down what you desire so it can support you in delivering it into your life experience—exactly as you wish.

This is the basis of the Law of Attraction, which states that what you focus on, you attract to you. So, the more specific details you can provide, the better.

If you're vague about what you want, you will get vague results.

Let's say you want to be...*happy*. What does that look like for *you*?

Lounging in a room full of Golden Retriever puppies who are licking your face?

Cruising down Mulholland Drive in LA in a flashy red Lamborghini?

Receiving a humanitarian award in front of a supportive crowd?

If you just said "I want to be happy" and left it at that, you could get the Lamborghini when you really wanted the award!

So, what are *you* hungry for? Specifically?

Spend some time contemplating that question. See what comes up for you. We'll circle back to that question very soon. In a few pages, I'll invite you to do a guided visualization so you can get really, really clear about what you're wishing for.

Before we get there, here's a little interlude...it's the story of how I made one of the biggest wishes of my life: the wish to build a brand new company, called Wishbeads.

The Download: How Wishbeads Was Born

Have you ever experienced that magic moment when everything comes in a flash—the big idea, the insight, the answer you've been waiting for. Boom! You're strolling through the park, or stuck in traffic, and suddenly an idea strikes you like lightning. It all pours into your brain. It's almost like you're downloading information from a mystical Wi-Fi signal in the sky—a giant file zipping straight into your heart from a master computer.

My company, Wishbeads, got downloaded just like that.

One morning, on a day that started out just like any other day, I was taking a shower. Between shampoo and conditioner, I heard the name "Wishbeads" and out of nowhere I could see the first product: a bracelet created from wishes written on paper, worn daily as a reminder to take action toward your deepest desires. In that same moment, I knew this piece of jewelry would become a vehicle to empower people across the globe. This little bracelet would help to make wishes come true. Even though I was in the middle of a hot, steamy shower, I got chills!

Before I go any further, it's important to understand a few events that happened just prior to my download from the Universe.

The first was a family trip to Lucca, Italy. We were celebrating my in-laws' fiftieth wedding anniversary. We spent a glorious week filled with endless hours of sightseeing, biking, and strolling the streets of this charming, ancient town.

One afternoon, we happened upon a craft fair in one of the piazzas. I was immediately drawn to an artist who was creating goods from paper and cloth, one of which was a collection of necklaces with beads made from rolled fabric and paper. When I saw them, I immediately stopped in my tracks. There was an unmistakable energy coming off of those necklaces that was inexplicably exciting to me.

I immediately purchased a few for myself and bunches for my friends. In the days that followed, I kept speaking about my newfound treasures and sharing my elation with all of my family members, who at one point expressed their bewilderment as to why I was so taken with these necklaces.

"Aren't they aaahhh-MAZ-ing?!" I would repeat over and over again.

A few weeks after I returned home to California, I was speaking about the necklaces with a good friend of mine who casually said, "You know Alexa, you could probably make them yourself."

So I got curious. Then I got crafty.

I'm the mother of two boys, so I must admit, crafting had been on the back burner for many, many years. I'm a tomboy by nature, so raising young lads inspired me to learn to throw a football with a mean spiral. I even started taking karate lessons from the children's Sensei. I'm more of jock now than when I was a teenager! Crafting was entirely off my radar.

I soon found myself cruising the aisles of Michael's and heading to the dollar store in search of supplies to create my own paper bead and fabric necklaces. I bought elastic, five types of Mod Podge, scraps of paper, fabric cuts offs and more. Sunday afternoons were filled with messes on the kitchen table. There was no purpose to this play. It was fun for fun's sake and I loved getting my hands dirty.

I glued wrapping paper, newspaper, and scraps of paper just laying around the house until I found just the right consistency for my liking. Sticky bliss.

Then came the second incident.

One night, I had the honor of spending the evening with an extraordinary group of women who were transitioning out of homelessness. I was a guest speaker at our local community center. That night I was sharing some insights about the power of positive thoughts and the energy of intention. I demonstrated how powerful a single positive thought can be on your entire body and how that energy can carry you through difficult times.

While I was standing in front of those brave women, I recognized how impossible their situations seemed to be—certainly in comparison to my own. I, by all rights, have had a very charmed life. There was a part of me that felt discussing the power of positive thoughts might be minimizing the reality that lay ahead of them. But I persisted.

I went on to explain how they can choose to focus their mind on a single object that inspires them—the sunset, a smile, a flower blooming—and that energy will help carry them through the moments of doubt and uncertainty that will inevitably arise. I encouraged them to visualize their future home and the security they so deserved. We spoke about faith. We spoke about personal power and the necessity of celebrating small wins along the way. The end result was an evening of laughter, connection, and hope.

The next morning in the shower, the two incidents came together as one and I received the download for Wishbeads.

I could see the product so clearly: a kit with all the supplies you need to create a bracelet with your wishes inside; like a vision board you wear on your wrist. By wearing the bracelet daily, you have a visual reminder to stay focused on what you want in life. Wishes. Beads. Put it together and you've got...Wishbeads. It was that simple.

My entrepreneurial mind immediately chimed in, *Yeah, right. Like the name Wishbeads will be available. That's so obvious, I'm sure it's already taken.*

I was still dripping wet when I ran to the computer and checked to see if, in fact, Wishbeads.com was available and—much to my amazement—it was. So was the trademark and all the social media handles.

Game on. Now it was time to make it happen.

Once the idea was hatched, it seemed inevitable that I would find a way to create this product. After all, this idea wouldn't have come to me if I wasn't somehow ready, willing, and able.

So I accepted the challenge.

Aaaand then I immediately felt overwhelmed and uncertain as to how to pull it off.

I thought to myself, *I don't know anything about making jewelry. I don't know anything about manufacturing a product. I've never done anything like this before. And besides, what if nobody even likes this product? What if I invest tons of time into this Wishbeads project and then I only sell...like, two bracelets? What if this whole idea is completely stupid and I burn through my savings and my family is bankrupt and I will have wasted all my time, all my money, all my effort and have absolutely nothing to show for it?! How could I face my kids?!*

I knew I had to shove aside all those voices of doubt and just...get to work. Just take the first tiny step. So that's what I did.

I looked up old friends who I vaguely recalled were in manufacturing. I reached out to contacts who had branding expertise and design experience. I started brainstorming the various ways I could bring this to the marketplace. All this while running a household, raising kids, coaching clients, teaching online, and having some semblance of a social life.

Wishbeads became my side hustle.

I found time here and there and in between it all to slowly build a prototype. Many months went by, and while I shared this concept with a trusted inner circle of friends, it was far from coming to life.

Enter...Oprah.

In April 2016, I had the good fortune of attending Oprah Winfrey's Super Soul Sessions at UCLA's Royce Hall in Los Angeles. She had assembled an all-star list of speakers including Eckhart Tolle, Cheryl Strayed, Marie Forleo, and more. I was in heaven.

Then India.Arie stepped on stage.

I wasn't familiar with her music, but I was immediately drawn in by her presence. She spoke about her mission to create "songversations" or dialogs through her music. Then she grabbed her guitar and sang an acoustic version of "I Am Light."

My entire body became electrified.

It was as if every cell in my being knew with certainty that the time was now to bring Wishbeads into the world—for real. When she finished her song, I turned to my friend Liv, and with the face of total conviction, said, "That's it. I MUST do Wishbeads... NOW."

Forty days later, I launched a Kickstarter campaign for Wishbeads that went on to raise twenty-five thousand dollars in thirty days.

I was off to the races.

What followed was months of building the foundation of a business. Funding, manufacturing, distribution, marketing, and creating Wishbeads bracelets with lots of incredible people. Six months after I launched the Wishbeads kit, I developed my next signature product: a beaded bracelet in a variety of stones, which features a brass cylinder where you stash your written wish. The same concept as the previous idea, but a tad simpler for customers to assemble.

Now with more ways to wish, there were more opportunities for people to make their wishes come true.

Was the process of launching the Wishbeads business always fun? Nope. *I'm not particularly fond of Excel spreadsheets.*

Was it what I expected? Hardly. *I actually had no idea what I was getting into, thank goodness.*

Was it work? Tons! Still is! But guess what? *I love what I'm learning, the people that I meet along the way, and the energy of making progress!*

Running the Wishbeads company has been (and still is) one of my greatest wishes.

Now let's talk about *you.*

What is *your* greatest wish?

Is it to become the CEO of your own company, like I did? Is it
to save up enough money to pursue a PhD without going into
debt? Is your biggest wish something health-related, like getting
strong enough to run a 10K race or do one-handed push-ups
like an action movie star? Maybe your biggest wish is to adopt a
puppy with a wagging tail? Or get a new job? Or meet an amazing
romantic partner? Or book a trip to Paris? Or maybe you're not
wishing for anything flashy or dramatic. Maybe right now, your
greatest wish is something really simple, like, "I want to wake up
and start each day feeling calm instead of feeling stressed. That's
my number one wish!"

At long last, we're getting into the really fun part of this book!
Keep reading and let's discuss how to set a highly specific wish—
the more specific, the better.

The Glossary: Important Words to Know

Before we mosey along, here are some important words and
phrases that I'll be using throughout this book. You might already
be familiar with these concepts, or you might not! It never hurts
to have a little refresher course...

Wish – A wish is something you desire, crave, or long to
experience in your life. The more specific you can be as you make
your wish, the better. For example, "I want to be fit" is fine, but
try to be more specific. For example, try saying: "I want to be fit
enough to run a 5K race, which I'll do while listening to a playlist
of my favorite music!"

Wishwork – Wishwork is a word that I made up. It's the work
that's required to make your wish come true. Depending on what

you're wishing for, the Wishwork might include practical steps (like putting together a website or booking a plane ticket) as well as emotional/spiritual steps (like changing your attitude about a situation) or both!

Inside this book, I map out twenty-one days of Wishwork for you to complete. If you follow along and do the work for twenty-one days in a row, you'll be amazed at what happens. You'll make so much progress toward making your wish come true. Daily action leads to...*results!*

Wishbeads – Wishbeads is a jewelry company that I started. We sell two different styles of bracelets. One style has a hollow compartment where you can tuck a wish inside. The other style has paper beads that are created from slips of paper. By wearing a Wishbeads bracelet on your wrist, you're wearing a daily reminder to keep working toward your dreams.

Law of Attraction – The Law of Attraction is a spiritual principle that many people believe (although some don't, and that's ok, because we're all entitled to our individual beliefs!). The Law of Attraction states that what we focus on, we attract. When we hold good thoughts and feelings, this positive energy attracts similar energy. In a practical sense, this means if you smile at people on the street, typically, they smile back. If you're generous with your friends, typically, they're generous with you in return. Whatever you put into the world tends to boomerang right back to you—at least, most of the time.

Energy – When people talk about your "energy," they usually mean your mood, your attitude, the vibe you give off. Consider when someone walks into a room and immediately they give off a sour, bitter, hostile energy. They don't even have to say a single word—their body language and facial expression says it all! Everyone in the room can feel this person's energy. The type of energy you put out into the world impacts how you are perceived, how you feel as you go about your day, and ultimately, the likelihood that you'll be able to make your wishes come true.

Visualization – A visualization is a meditative experience where you close your eyes, breathe deeply, and then allow a picture to unfold inside your mind's eye. It might be a photo, a drawing, or even a movie that plays out, like watching a story unfold onscreen. Doing a visualization is another way of saying "using your imagination." Many people find that visualizing is a great way to reduce anxiety, quiet down the chattering noise inside your mind, think more clearly, and identify solutions you hadn't seen before.

Manifest – The word manifest means to make something real, to bring something into existence. If someone says, "I manifested this new apartment!" what they probably mean is, "I wished for this new apartment, I took action to make my wish come true, and now—hooray—I've got the home of my dreams!"

Universe – People describe the Universe in thousands of different ways. This is my personal definition: the Universe is a loving, benevolent force that wants you to succeed and be happy—and that wants to help make your wishes come true. You might prefer a term like God, Goddess, Gaia, Love, Spirit, Oneness, or some other phrase. Throughout this book, I usually stick with Universe. (But feel free to mentally swap that word for any word that you prefer.)

Negative Mindset – Having a negative mindset means you're choosing to see the world through a negative, pessimistic lens. It means believing that most people are bad, selfish, or "out to get you" in some way, and that hard work is pointless because everything's unfair. Even when wonderful things happen—like winning a scholarship or meeting a new friend—when you've got a negative mindset, you will find a way to twist the situation into something dark, or even sabotage your own success. You'll decide, "The scholarship isn't big enough, I need several thousand more," or "She probably only wants to be my friend because she wants me to do a big favor for her." People who choose to have a negative mindset often struggle to make their wishes come true, which further reinforces their belief that "the world is unfair."

Positive Mindset – Having a positive mindset means you're choosing to see the world through a positive, optimistic lens. It means believing that most people are good, that hard work usually pays off, and that the Universe wants all of us to be happy, to not suffer. Even when painful things happen, like death, illness, catastrophes, or senseless acts of violence, someone who has cultivated a positive mindset will always try to find the "good" in any situation. For example, if a tsunami strikes and wrecks a seaside town, someone with a positive mindset might say, "This is awful news, however, it's beautiful to see everyone rallying together to raise money and repair buildings and donate supplies. People can be so strong and resilient. I'm so inspired by what I'm seeing and I'll do my part to help out, too!"

Make a Wish

SEE YOUR WISH

Sometimes, wishes feel very obvious. If someone asks, "What's your greatest wish?" you might immediately say, "Finding a better job" or "Going to Hawaii next summer for a surfing vacation." Boom. Clear and simple.

But sometimes, we have wishes that aren't *quite* so obvious. Wishes we're not fully aware of, at first. They're almost like *secret* wishes, *quiet* wishes, buried deep down in our hearts, waiting patiently to be noticed. Sometimes these are the most important wishes of all—the ones that bring the greatest fulfillment.

How do you discover these kinds of wishes?

I've found that the best way to discover this kind of wish is to slow down, close your eyes, quiet your mind, and allow your inner being to *show* you a vision of what you secretly desire. (This is called "doing a visualization" or "visualizing.")

In this meditative place, you can invite a scenario to unfold in your mind's eye where you are witnessing your wish as if it has already come true. A moment in time—at some point in the future—when you are living your wish.

Visualizing your wish is the first step in the Wishwork journey. It's an experience that can be done on your own, or with someone guiding you along, depending on your preference.

(Good news: I've recorded a guided visualization for you...and I'll share the link to that audio file in a moment! You can listen and follow along.)

*First time trying a visualization? Worried you're not going to be
"good" at this?*

If you don't meditate or visualize regularly, or if you've never tried
this type of thing before, that's ok! Everyone can do this. You
don't need any special skills.

Just give yourself some quiet time to explore this in your own
way. You can listen to great music, close your eyes and allow
words or feelings to emerge. You can sit down and do some
automatic writing, where you don't stop writing until all your
ideas are on the page. Write without judging or censoring
yourself—just using your intuition and allowing yourself to
explore with language.

In this relaxed, reflective place, you go beyond wishing for
things. (We all have too much material stuff anyway.) You allow
yourself to witness a moment in time when you feel completely
and utterly content. This state of being is filled with positive
emotions, positive environments, and sometimes other positive
people.

Visualizing brings you...new clues.

When you close your eyes and do a visualization, and allow
yourself to see your greatest wish, you will see all kinds of *tiny
clues*—clues about what you really want, and why, and how to
make your wish come true.

For instance...

Seeing a table full of delicious food might be a clue that you want
to spend more time with friends and family, and may inspire you
to try new recipes, host a dinner party, and make more time
to cook.

Seeing a scenario where you are holding the hand of a little girl while you walk down the beach may awaken you to the idea that you wish to have a family in addition to the career you have been pursuing so passionately for years. In response, you may make time to have important conversations with friends and family, make space in your calendar for more personal time, or ask friends about their experiences as parents.

Seeing yourself at the head of a conference table, grounded, calm, and confident as you deliver a presentation, may awaken you to step into a new type of leadership in your company. You may be inspired to speak with your boss, seek additional training, or simply trust that you have the skills needed to shine at work.

When you see yourself experiencing your wish—as if it's already come true—you set the wheels in motion for making it happen.

You see it, you write it down (and the Universe takes note!) and then you do the work.

It's easier than you think.

A Guided Visualization

It's time to begin. Let's set the stage for your success.

First, carve out some time for yourself—either alone or with a circle of friends who are committed to doing this experience together. Book the time, keep the distractions away, and give yourself the gift of making time to wish.

Second, make sure you have a comfortable place to sit or lie down and something to write with—a notebook and pen, a laptop, whatever you prefer to use. You can also "set the scene" and make the environment feel beautiful with flowers, candles, and perhaps a window cracked open to allow fresh air to flow in. Make the space feel good to you.

All set? Got everything you need? Just before you begin your visualization, I recommend listening to a song that moves your spirit and quiets your mind. "I Am Light" by India.Arie is a personal favorite of mine. But you can pick whatever song you want.

Listen to the song. Then, when it's over, allow the silence to help you relax so you can settle your thoughts and get very present.

Once you're ready, go to wishbeads.com/yes to download a guided visualization that I've recorded for you. Play the audio. Close your eyes and listen.

Or, if you're with a friend, you can ask your friend to read the visualization aloud to you. Here's the text for them to read...

> *Imagine an orb of light in the center of your chest. It can be whatever color you wish. As you breathe in, imagine this ball of light growing bigger and as you gently exhale, it's growing bigger still. This light has always been within you—ever since you were born. It's the seat of your spirit, your intuition, and your greatest wishes. When you connect your mind to this light, a feeling of peace and calm washes over you.*
>
> *As you breathe in and out, this light grows so bright that it shines outward, like an old movie projector, shining a scene on a giant screen in front of you. In this scene, you are experiencing your wish.*
>
> *Now, step into this scene and allow yourself to be in that moment—this special moment that you will*

experience at some point in the future—where you are living your wish. Awaken your senses in this time and place and see if you can identify and articulate how you feel.

What words would you use to describe this feeling? Remember those words.

Walk around in this time and place. What do you hear? Remember those sounds.

See if you can touch some objects in this time and place. What can you pick up? Remember how they felt.

What are you doing in this time and place? Remember your actions.

Where are you? See if you can notice subtle details. Remember as many specifics as possible.

Who are you with? Notice if you're alone or with others. Remember those around you.

With every detail comes deeper insights into what your being truly desires...

After you feel that you have absorbed this experience as deeply as possible, slowly bring yourself back to the present moment. Allow yourself to wiggle your fingers and toes and slowly open your eyes to gently bring your awareness into your body. Take your time.

Write It Down

What did you "see" while your eyes were closed? Write it down.

When you're ready, grab your notebook or laptop or whatever you're using and write down as many details as you can recall. The more specific you are, the better.

Write down whatever you saw during your visualization in the *present tense*, as if you are living inside of that moment *right now.* Use phrases like "I am," "I have," "I notice," "I feel."

For example, you could write down, "I am sitting in a cabin in the woods and there's a crackling fire. The kids are roasting s'mores and I am wearing cozy socks." That's present tense language. You're writing as if it's all happening right now! Write like that, rather than "I would like to be at a cabin in the woods" or "I wish I was relaxing inside a cabin" or "What I saw during my visualization was a cozy cabin." Try to stay in the present tense.

It's all happening...now.

You've seen your wish. You've experienced it. You've felt it. You've written about it as if it's already happened. You can go back to it in your mind's eye anytime you want. It's your wish. It's already a part of you. Now all you have to do is stay focused and work toward it through small, daily exercises, which I call *Wishwork*.

By focusing on your Wishwork for the next twenty-one days, you are building a healthy new habit. For three weeks, you are training your mind to keep your wish front and center, so you can remember what's important to you and your happiness. When you do anything for twenty-one days, you develop a habit that sticks.

After twenty-one days...will your wish come true? Perhaps! Or maybe not. Some wishes are simple. Some wishes are *huge*. Some wishes involve governments and the weather. Some wishes depend on a subtle shift in awareness. In other words, every wish is unique and your ability to make your wishes come true *begins* with understanding (and seeing for yourself!) how powerful you are to manifest what you want in your life. You'll see synchronicities. You'll feel the energy of curiosity and wonder. You'll see for yourself that staying positive and proactive simply feels better than believing you'll never get what you want. The more effort you put in, the more likely you'll see results. Be patient, stay open, and have fun with the process.

While it may be tempting to read through this book cover to cover in one go, the real magic comes from the daily commitment for twenty-one days.

In addition to this book, you can also download the free Wishbeads app (visit the App Store on your phone) to help you stay on track. Every day, you can listen to a personal audio message from me. You can even set daily notifications, so you never miss a day.

Are you ready to dive in and get started? I bet you are. Happy wishing!

Do the Work

"WORK" IS NOT A BAD WORD

When you hear the word "work," do your shoulders slump down, eyelids get heavy, and do you feel like crawling back in bed? Work gets a bad reputation as something you do to make money and pay the bills so you can get back to your pizza and Netflix.

But work doesn't have to be tedious, difficult, and endless.

Let's take flossing.

The act of flossing your teeth is so simple. Just a little waxed thread, applied gently between your teeth once or twice a day will leave your gums pink and healthy and your pearly whites plaque free. This ninety-second routine can prevent disease, help you avoid oral surgery, and even keep your teeth from falling out. Oh, the benefits are OBVIOUS!

And yet...many reports suggest that only 30 percent of the American population flosses regularly. Not only that, according to a survey conducted by the American Academy of Periodontology, 27 percent of the American population lies to their dentist about their flossing habits!

Such a wee bit of work, for such a massive investment in future happiness!

So, why don't most people do such a simple task—even when they know the obvious rewards?

I believe it comes down to an issue of trust. Trusting that simple, daily efforts will pay off over time.

Life can be complicated and noisy and it's all too easy to feel pulled in many directions. What with the demands of your calendar and fitting in time for family, friends, other obligations, and the demands of work—everyone wanting a response every minute of the day, with alerts beeping at you all day long—it's no wonder we short-change ourselves by neglecting the simple tasks that enrich our lives and make us healthier and happier.

When was the last time you took a stroll in your neighborhood?

When was the last time you watched a sunset?

When was the last time you helped a stranger?

Tiny moments of joy are available to us all the time. They're free! They're easy! They're right in front of our faces!

And yet...we don't prioritize the very things that make us feel calm, connected, and content. We don't trust that we can walk away from our to-do lists to be present to the magic that's all around us. We don't trust the impact it will have on our lives and the lives of others.

You are about to embark on a journey that may seem wildly simple. So simple in fact that you may not think it's "work" at all.

Every day—for twenty-one days—you are invited to see the world a little bit differently. You are encouraged to take a very small step. You are asked to reflect on what you experienced during the day and write about it at night. You might say, "This is too easy. Sure, I am doing the 'Wishwork' every day, but is this really helping to make my wish come true? Is anything happening?"

Trust that it is. It's all happening for you. Just like flossing your teeth, these simple, daily habits really do pay off!

By doing the Wishwork, you will manifest what you desire. You will feel the shift. You will experience the coincidences. You will see for yourself...that wishes really do come true.

Are you ready to begin twenty-one days of Wishwork?

First, have you visualized your wish? Yes? Excellent! Proceed to the next page! No? Not yet? You skipped that part? No problem. Turn back to the section of this book called "See Your Wish" and do the guided visualization exercise so that you can see your wish clearly—with all of its beautiful details. Once you've done that, away we go! It's time to take twenty-one small, daily steps and work toward making your wish come true! Let's go!

21 Days of Wishwork

DAY 1: TIME TO SMILE

Today your Wishwork begins.

Today you are saying YES to taking action.

Today you are stepping into a new way of seeing the world.

And big changes begin with the simplest gestures.

Your SMILE.

When you smile, your body creates delicious "feel-good" chemicals. Dopamine, serotonin, and endorphins begin cascading through your bloodstream. Your heart rate slows down, your blood pressure drops, and you instantly feel a deeper sense of calm.

Not only that, when you smile at someone else, it triggers them to do the same, causing a positive chain reaction of goodness! In one study in Sweden, researchers noticed that participants would unconsciously mimic facial expressions when seeing pictures of various emotions. Despite being told to frown when looking at a smiling face, they couldn't help but smile. Their cingulate cortex, the part of their brain responsible for subconscious emotional mimicry, automatically triggered their smile before they could remember the instructions. Our body reacts before our mind can intervene.

In our busy lives, it's all too easy to bury our faces in our phones, our to-do lists, and our preoccupied minds, but making your wishes come true requires "miraculous" moments of connection, both with yourself and with others.

A smile uplifts your energy so when you walk into a room, people naturally want to be around you.

A smile is an invitation for strangers to look you in the eye.

A smile tells your body and mind to stay open and optimistic about life.

Your smile unlocks *your secret superpower*—an energy inside you that lifts you up and makes the world take notice.

Today it's time to smile and see what unfolds as a result.

WITNESS: A smile is a spark of joy. The more you see, the more you get. Notice as many smiles today as you can. Hint: You can make someone smile simply by smiling at them.

WRITE: Name three things today that made you smile. How did they make you feel? How could that energy help you achieve your wish?

DAY 2: STIR THE SOUL

Earlier in this book, I invited you to do a visualization—to close your eyes, use your imagination, and "see" a moment in time when your wish has already come true.

While my friend Kim was doing a visualization, a picture emerged of her at home, moments before her son returned from school. She saw herself sitting at her desk, writing on her computer. For her, she knew what that moment meant.

She was home—not hustling all over town in late night meetings.

She was there—ready to greet her son when he came home instead of him walking into an empty apartment.

She was at her desk—quietly creating her own work and schedule.

It was a glimpse of a different life—an opportunity to embark on a new career path and a chance to finally begin her passion project: a young adult book series to spark a nationwide community service initiative.

Inspired by this vision, she started taking immediate steps. After work, she researched outside projects she could get involved with. She spoke with an accountant about starting up her own business. She carved out some extra time to sit down and write her book.

A few short months later, she made her vision her reality. Her consultant business was up and running, the first draft of the book was finished, and she loved deciding her own hours.

And yet, so much change in so little time inevitably created moments of doubt.

It was after she had created her second Wishbeads bracelet, this time envisioning the success of her new book, that she experienced the power of the Wishwork. Day Two is an invitation to listen to music as a messenger. That morning, she turned on the radio in her car and heard the familiar voice of Tom Petty but it was a song she had never heard before or at least couldn't remember hearing: "Louisiana Rain."

> *Louisiana rain is falling at my feet*
> *Baby I'm noticing the change as I move down the street*
> *Louisiana rain is soaking through my shoes*
> *I may never be the same when I reach Baton Rouge*

Tears started filling her eyes. She was born and raised in Louisiana. Her parents had passed away a few years earlier, and in that moment, she felt their presence, encouraging her to keep going.

It was just the words she needed to hear, as if her folks were whispering them in her ear.

As you move along your journey, working on making your wish come true, it's important to surround yourself with positive messages—messages that remind you that you're on the right path, and that remind you to keep going, to keep taking that next step. Music is a fabulous way to saturate yourself with the messages that you need. We all have certain songs that just "speak" to us, songs that stir the soul. Go find yours.

WITNESS: Music can be a messenger. Today turn on the radio, pop on a streaming station, or hit your playlist and randomly see what song is playing. Is there meaning for you? Does it stir your soul? When I was growing up, the highest form of flattery (and flirtation) was receiving a mix tape from a special someone. Why were those songs chosen? What was the special hidden meaning? Hmm...

WRITE: Tonight, write a list of special songs that inspire you to take action toward your wish. What music lifts your soul, helps you get your groove on, and makes you feel unstoppable? Make a list and then go ahead and create your very own playlist of tunes. Listen often. Music is such a powerful way to shift your mood. With a positive mood, you're far more likely to keep working toward making your wish come true!

DAY 3: THE PURITY OF GAZING

I remember the first time I saw someone riding a bike while clutching a chunky mobile phone. It was 1995 and I thought it was the craziest thing in the world.

What?! Are you kidding me? I thought to myself, my mouth agape at the absurdity of ruining a perfectly good bike ride.

A few years later, working at a coffee shop, I stood horrified when someone absentmindedly paused their cell call to place an order.

Today, it's unusual to see anyone *not* drowning in a device.

Life, in all of its subtle deliciousness, is happening all around you, but when was the last time you paused to notice...

- The way the breeze feels on your cheeks.

- The sound of the birds chirping in the trees.

- The distant laughter of kids playing ball in the park.

Mindfulness is a practice that reconnects you to yourself and the world around you. Today is your invitation to gaze. Softly see the details. Take the time to awaken your senses. Resist the temptation to grab your phone. Gaze at life instead. It's kind of miraculous.

When you are connected to yourself and to the world around you—instead of distractedly staring at Instagram or Facebook—your wish is more likely to come true.

WITNESS: Children stare. Animals stare. Their gazes are genuine, without judgment, and as long as they need to be. Today, gaze softly at something. Or see if you can spot someone else gazing. Just witness it and see how it makes you feel.

WRITE: Tonight, before you go to bed, take a moment and gently gaze at yourself in the mirror. No judgment. Just compassion and love. Write down what this experience feels like for you. Does it feel awkward? Does it feel natural? Know this: the more you can gaze at yourself in a compassionate way, the better (and more confident) you feel, and the easier it becomes to make your wishes come true.

DAY 4: BOOK IT

Procrastination can be a beast. Of course we *want* to get things finished—on schedule. It's just all too easy to push our tasks off for another day. Nobody has a PhD in time management (*do they?*), nor do you need one to overcome the urge to put off doing something, but taking a *single tiny action* is the first step in overcoming procrastination once and for all.

When you commit to accomplishing *one tiny thing*, you:

- Kick perfectionism to the curb.

- Silence the voice of doubt in your head by showing your inner naysayer who's boss.

- Build a new habit of tackling the things that matter the most first.

What's that sneaky task that's been spinning in your head, sucking up valuable energy? What tiny little thing have you been putting off doing, that you could knock out this very morning?

Setting up an appointment to your dermatologist to get that funky mole looked at?

Mailing that package back so you can get a refund?

Tossing that spoiled bag of kale lingering in the veggie drawer?

One tiny thing off your to-do list makes you feel like a superhero, ready to tackle more and more each day. You feel better. You get stuff done. You show the Universe, *Hey, I'm ready, willing and able to TAKE ACTION toward what I want.*

Action = Results. Do it today.

WITNESS: Look at your calendar or to-do list for today. Gaze with intention at *one tiny thing* that you are determined to accomplish today. How will you feel once it's finished?

WRITE: Open your calendar for six months from now and make an "appointment" for something related to your wish. Book it! Maybe it's "Leave for road trip" or "Meeting with book agent" or "Ask my boss for a raise." Really, actually write it into your calendar, like it's a real appointment that you cannot miss! Show yourself that you're serious about this.

DAY 5: FOCUS ON OTHERS

Have you ever considered how exhausting it is to constantly be focusing on yourself? Endlessly replaying conversations in your head, second-guessing what you're wearing when you step in front of the mirror, and doubting whether or not the person in front of you finds you fascinating—all of this fretting drains you and immediately takes you out of the moment, robbing you of experiencing the richness of life.

When you're lucky enough to be face to face with another human being, take advantage of it! The moment you focus on them, you free yourself from your relentless inner chatter. Like magic, you begin to:

- Notice tiny details—about the person and the stories they share.

- Get really present—helping you calm your nerves and get grounded.

- Develop empathy for others—by understanding their perspective more deeply.

Not long ago, I was having one of those days where my mind felt stretched in a zillion directions. I was packing my suitcase, getting ready to fly to New York City to showcase Wishbeads at a big trade show—a huge opportunity that I didn't want to mess up. Meanwhile, my clients needed some attention. My dog needed to be walked. My inbox was crammed with unanswered emails. I felt "behind" on tons of things. My mind was full of anxious chatter: *You've loaded too many things onto your plate, Alexa! You've bitten off more than you can chew! You'll never get caught up!*

I took a deep breath. I set a new intention: *For the rest of today, I am going to stop focusing on myself—and my busy workload—and instead, focus on other people.* I focused on my kids—their sweet faces, the way it felt when they hugged me goodbye as I left for the airport, the sound of their voices saying, "I love you, mom." I focused on my cab driver's face, the crinkles by his eyes, the music he played during our ride. I focused on the flight attendant and made sure to give her a genuine smile and say "thank you" when she handed me a beverage.

Focusing on other people shifted my whole day. It put me back into a positive frame of mind so that I could waltz into the NYC tradeshow, feeling confident and grounded, and do a terrific job—instead of feeling nervous and scattered. This is the power of shifting your focus.

Life is noisy, but your mind doesn't have to be. Today, I invite you to focus on others and you will see what I mean. Everyone wins.

WITNESS: Listening is a gift. Can you find a moment today to really stop and listen to someone? Focus on someone else. Give them your undivided attention for at least five minutes. See their eyes. Hear their voice. Quiet your thoughts. What difference do you experience as a result?

WRITE: What discoveries did you make about yourself as a listener today? Where did you find inner resistance? When was it easy for you? How do you think this skill will help you manifest your wish?

DAY 6: BEING, NOT DOING

Oh, the mighty to-do list. We fill it with chores, goals, and reminders. Tasks for the day. Reminders for the week. Goals for the year. It's a neverending game of checking off and adding on. A game that never seems to let up steam, leaving us exhausted by its mere existence.

In all of that *doing*, we rarely set time for BEING.

Focusing our efforts on any given activity creates results, but sometimes we accomplish more when we *release*.

Take crossword puzzles for example. When you sit down to do a new crossword puzzle, your mind focuses on finding all the possible answers. You hit the easy ones, then work really hard to figure out the ones that intersect those answers. You sip your coffee, scratch away at your folded newspaper (I'm old-fashioned!) and see how far you can get at that first pass. When you hit the wall—and can't possibly figure out any more clues—you put it down.

That's when your crossword brain starts to work its magic.

In letting go of the effort of *doing* the crossword, your brain is processing the information without you putting any attention on it whatsoever. While you are busy with life, a part of your mind is noodling 18A and 36D. When you do finally pick up your crossword puzzle a few days later—BOOM—you fill in more answers.

When you release the effort, your being takes over—allowing your mind, body, and spirit to work as one to help you discover answers you didn't think you knew. When you let go, you come back refreshed and ready to discover things from a new perspective.

In other words, when you're *relaxed*—not forcing, not straining, just being—you're more likely to have brilliant ideas and figure out how to make your wish come true. A brilliant title for your next essay. A brilliant name for your new product. A brilliant idea on how to raise funds for your next family vacation. Bam! These gems pop into your mind when you're allowing yourself to just… *be*.

WITNESS: Could you take some time today to stop doing-doing-doing and just…*be*? Take a hot shower, take a two-minute meditation break, or take a moment to sit outside and do absolutely nothing at all. Just be. Notice what happens. You might feel calmer. You might feel more grounded. Your brain might even surprise you with an *"a ha!"* moment—a solution to a problem you've been wrestling with for weeks.

WRITE: What's one simple adjustment you can do that will make your journey to achieving your wish a little easier? Get eight hours of sleep? Take a long walk to clear your head? Book a massage? Devote some time to journaling? Decide on one thing and take action to make it happen.

DAY 7: GREEN MEANS GO

Go-getters. They're people who seize opportunities, overcome obstacles, and relentlessly push forward. They have an idea, they take action. If they want to ask someone out on a date, they pick up the phone. When a prospective client says no, they pursue three new leads that same day.

In other words, they see green lights, even when the world presents a stop sign.

My mother, Billie, has a zest for life that is utterly contagious. The older she gets, the more outrageous her clothes, the more spin classes she attends, and the more countries she visits. She has the spirit and energy of a seventeen-year-old! I recall the day she was doing Day 7 of the Wishwork and we were following her downtown to see an exhibit at the Museum of Contemporary Art in downtown Los Angeles.

My car pulled up to hers at a light and she yelled, "One hundred and sixty-seven, baby! That's how many green lights I've seen today! Woohoo!" She then hit the gas the moment the light changed and pulled out in front of me, laughing.

One of the many lessons she's taught me is that life wants you to *win*. You didn't come to this planet to suffer, you came to experience a journey in which you get to discover who you really are, what you really want, and how you can make a difference in the world by being here.

When you cultivate a positive outlook on life, you actively seek *signs* that all is well. You train your mind toward what you want, instead of what's getting in your way.

You see green, not red.

WITNESS: For the rest of today, pay attention to the "green lights" that show up in your life. Look for literal green lights—at a traffic intersection, for example—and look for metaphorical green lights, too. Look for signs that whisper, "Go!" A door being propped open for you. A breeze blowing you forward. A photograph of a wide open road with no impediments in sight. An email that begins with "Yes!" How many green lights can you count today?

WRITE: Today, how did you feel when you focused on the energy of "green" and "go"? Extra credit: write down a couple things that have happened in your life recently that felt like green lights. Invitations. Opportunities. Yeses. Helping hands. Write down as many green lights as you can recall. At the bottom of your list, write a little note of gratitude. Something like: "Thank you, Universe, for showing me all of these green lights!"

DAY 8: IMPERFECTLY PERFECT

It's all too easy to focus on the things that drain our energy. Lousy traffic. Spilled coffee. Depressing news. We see it, feel it, and it immediately brings us down.

When I was first navigating the crowded streets of Los Angeles, I could feel my blood pressure rising as the 405 freeway became jammed with cars. What should have been a thirty-minute drive turned into a two hour brake-a-thon.

I would sit, stewing in my seat, infuriated that I was "wasting" so much time. Consequently, every time I set out to an audition, ran to an appointment, or simply tried to meet friends for dinner across town, I was filled with dread.

When I realized this habit, I stopped in my tracks. My reaction to this obstacle was bringing me down, not lifting me up. I changed my narrative from "LA traffic sucks" to "Goodie! I get to chill in my car—listen to music, hear an audio book, or call a friend and catch up." Suddenly, my car rides rejuvenated me instead of beating me up.

In Japan, there's a philosophy called *wabi-sabi*, which celebrates the beauty of imperfection. Many Japanese potters express *wabi-sabi* through the art of *kintsugi*, which is where you take a broken ceramic bowl and glue it back together, filling in the cracks with shimmering gold. The end result is a bowl that's cracked and flawed—yet somehow, even more beautiful than the "perfect" original.

Traffic isn't good or bad—*it merely is*—and our perspective *about* it creates our experience *of* it.

When we can embrace the "flaws" of life, we can appreciate everything on an entirely new level.

- The creativity of a room strewn with Legos.

- The passionate debate of a political discourse.

- The deeper awareness born from a miscommunication.

- There's beauty in the mess.

To make your wish come true, you need to become the type of person who sees beauty everywhere, not the type of person who sees obstacles, frustration, and disaster everywhere. You get to choose who you are going to be.

WITNESS: Today, pay attention to one thing you perceive as "flawed." It could be a pesky employee. A stain on your favorite shirt. An impossibly long hold time on the customer service line. Just one "flawed" thing. Notice how it makes you feel. See if you can pause in the moment and ask yourself, "Why does this bug me?"

Also, see if there's a way for you to shift your perspective about this. Maybe the tomato sauce stain on your favorite shirt is there because you were cooking up a storm, making a beautiful meal for your family, and things got a little wild in the kitchen! Reframe this "flaw" in a new light.

WRITE: When you think about the work that's required to make your wish come true, is there any part of the process that feels "bad" or "flawed" or even "broken"? For instance, "I wish to write a book, but my computer keeps freezing up" or "My wish is to save ten thousand dollars, but it's just going to take too long!" See if you can reframe this "flaw" in a new way. Can you look at this problem from a different perspective? Can you find the beauty in the flaw?

DAY 9: THE VOICE YOU CAN TRUST

About two thousand five hundred years ago, Buddha was traveling the countryside, sharing his insights with those he encountered. One day a villager asked, "We hear many sages, why should we listen to you and not the others?"

Buddha smiled and replied, "You will know the right path for you, if you follow your heart."

But following your heart is easier said than done, right? The voice of the heart—the inner voice, the true voice—often gets drowned out in the noisiness of life.

Back when I worked as an actress, I tried to follow my heart—but sometimes it felt difficult. My life was saturated with so many other voices: my agents, various directors, producers, and co-workers on set. Everyone had strong opinions about how I ought to perform, how I could further my career, even how I should dress and what my body should look like. While most of these people had the best of intentions, many days, it was difficult to quiet my mind and ask, "But what feels true...for me?"

As the years passed, I developed new skills—like meditating, journaling, or simply taking one deep breath—and these tools made it easier to get quiet and hear what my heart was trying to say.

It takes courage to trust your own voice...to trust your voice even more than you trust the voices of "mentors" and "experts" and other people around you. Because ultimately, you, and only you, are the true expert on your own life.

Ask yourself:

- What makes me happy?

- What brings me contentment?

- What's one thing I know for sure about myself?

- Do I trust my inner voice, or do I tend to look elsewhere to collect other people's opinions?

- If so, what might be causing me to doubt my own instincts?

- When does my mind feel noisy and cluttered?

- When does my mind feel quiet and clear?

When you quiet your mind, you can hear your inner voice more clearly—the wise inner voice that knows exactly how you can make your wish come true, the inner voice with instructions for you.

WITNESS: See if you can find a moment today where you "hear" your inner voice. When did you get a flash of insight? What did your inner voice tell you? How did you respond?

WRITE: Tonight, record your experience from today. How can you begin to trust that inner voice just a little bit more? How can you invite your inner voice to be just a little bit louder? Is there anything that your inner voice has been telling you lately—any instructions about what you need to do to get your wish?

DAY 10: MENTALLY REHEARSE

When was the last time you took a deep dive into the world of imagination?

One Saturday morning a few weeks ago, the house was unusually quiet. Some birds were chirping in the trees just outside the kitchen, my dog was curled up in bed, and my boys were in the living room chatting in hushed tones.

I admit, I was a bit suspicious. I walked in expecting to see a plot hatching or faces buried in Minecraft. Instead, I saw them totally immersed in their own LEGO worlds. Intricate spaceships flying through the air, expansive cityscapes complete with a mini mart and a two-story police station and some drama unfolding with a fire truck and a helicopter.

They were captivated and totally unaware of my presence...*for hours*.

As we get older, we take on lots of responsibilities, leaving little time for imaginative play, creative exploration, and conscious daydreaming. We're busy, right?

But did you know that when you activate your imagination, you are firing up critical neutrons in your brain that help you become a more creative thinker?

When you picture a scenario in which your wish has come true, you're *broadening your sense of perception*—expanding your awareness beyond the actual experiences you've had, to plant the seeds for the future you wish to experience.

Researchers who study human behavior have found some fascinating connections between what we "imagine" and how we actually "perform" in everyday life. Google the phrase "mental practice—research" and you'll see many studies that have been done in recent years.

One famous study shows that people who imagine practicing the piano—imagining their fingers hitting the correct keys—actually perform better, with fewer mistakes, once they sit down at a real piano to play. Amazing, right? Using their imagination, they are "mentally rehearsing" for the real thing—literally, reshaping their brain to create the reality they want.

We can use our imaginations to mentally rehearse in all realms of life—not just playing the piano. When you imagine you're running fast and crossing the finish line, imagine yourself stepping onstage with confidence to give a presentation, imagine yourself opening the doors of your new bakery, imagine yourself building a new home or business or garden, whatever you imagine, you're laying down new pathways in your brain to help make it happen... for real.

See it. Feel it. Become it.

WITNESS: Think about a specific task that you need to do this week. Something you'd like to do well, with joy and confidence. It could be baking bread, meeting with a client, or enjoying quality time with a friend. With your eyes closed, imagine that moment—visualize it unfolding in the most beautiful possible way. Mentally rehearse for that moment. In doing so, you're bringing this wish into being.

WRITE: Spend five minutes daydreaming about how your life will feel and look once your greatest wish comes true. Mentally rehearse how it's going to feel once you're "there." Then write down how it feels using present tense language, like: "I am," "I have," "I see," "It feels like..."

DAY 11: FOCUS ON THE WINS!

What you focus on...expands.

You've probably experienced this before, right?

Considering buying a Prius? *Suddenly the freeway is full of them.*

Curious about being vegan? *You notice a new vegan restaurant on every block.*

Pondering adopting a pet? *Every neighbor seems to be walking a new dog.*

You tune your mind toward an idea and BOOM—suddenly, it's appearing everywhere in your life.

You have this incredible superpower: *to focus on what you want and manifest what your mind desires.* And yet, most people spend their days doing the exact opposite! Instead of focusing on what we want—the goal, the victory, the big win, the sweet reward—we focus on everything we *don't* want.

We focus on everything that feels irritating. We get worked up over obnoxious drivers, long lines at the airport, restaurant servers who move a little too slowly, and annoying telemarketing calls. When we turn our attention toward these annoyances, pretty soon, life feels like a drag instead of a gift.

If you find yourself slipping into a pattern of irritation and annoyance, it's time to change your point of focus. Remember, what you choose to focus on is entirely up to you! And whatever you focus on, that's what's going to expand in your life.

Forget the person who cut you off in traffic. Focus on the amazing podcast you're listening to in the car!

Ignore the inbox crammed with spam. Instead, choose to be grateful for the email inquiry you received from a prospective client!

Why focus on life's frustrations, when you can choose to focus on life's *wins*?

When you acknowledge how your day has gone *right*—no matter how small the win—you take back your personal power. You reinforce good feelings. You feel empowered to make your wishes come true.

Little victories are all around us, every day. Tune in. Focus on them. The more you focus on the wins, the more wins start piling up.

WITNESS: Notice the "tiny wins" today. Your kids get dressed without being asked. Score! A friend returns your call and you have a lovely chat. Nice! You find five dollars in your back pocket. Sweet! Keep track. How many wins can you count?

WRITE: It's so easy to focus on all the wishes that haven't come true yet. Today (and hopefully every day going forward) do the opposite. Focus on the wishes that *did* come true. Can you think of three wishes you made—in the past—that actually came true? Write them down. Take a moment to read each one back to yourself. Smile and say to yourself (and to the Universe), "Whoa, seriously...thank you."

DAY 12: SAY IT

For most of her life, a client of mine named Deja *never* talked about money. Not with her family. Not with her friends. Not even with her fiancé. She struggled with money in various ways, but she never told anyone or sought help. Her parents hadn't ever talked about money when she was growing up, so she was raised with a "don't ask, don't tell, just don't bring it up" attitude toward financial matters.

But Deja had a secret wish: she wanted to make more money. Not just a little more money. *A lot more.* She wanted to make six figures by the end of the year.

Deja bought a Wishbeads bracelet, wrote down her wish, and started wearing her wish on her wrist. She also started doing the twenty-one-day Wishwork process, recording her observations and feelings in her journal. On Day 12, she saw today's prompt— *Say It*—and she knew it was time to overcome her fear of talking about money. It was time to put her wish out into the world for someone to hear.

A few hours later, she found herself at a coffee shop and started chatting with the next person in line. The woman noticed her Polished Black Onyx Wishbeads bracelet and commented how much she liked it. She quietly realized that this was her big chance to share her wish. So she did.

"Actually, this is my Wishbeads bracelet and I have a big wish this year... I wrote it and it's inside this cylinder. Well...today I had this crazy assignment where I have to tell a stranger my wish... So, I'm working on a plan to earn six figures this year!" Deja blurted out. It felt a bit awkward but she was so thrilled to say the words!

By the end of the day, she told practically everyone else in her life.

By the end of the year, her wish came true.

It's incredible what happens when we clarify exactly what we want, write it down, wear it, live it, work on it, and *say it* to other people, too. Sometimes saying your wish aloud is the hardest part. But I urge you to be brave and do it. Just watch what happens next.

WITNESS: Today, tell three people about your wish. Tell your barista, your neighbor, or maybe even your spouse. If you're feeling brave, post about it on social media. Say it to the world!

WRITE: Well, what happened? How did you feel? How did other people respond? Do you feel a shift (more excitement, more energy, a new spring in your step) now that the truth is out in the world?

DAY 13: YOU'RE DOING GREAT

Has something like this ever happened to you?

You give a presentation at work and it goes pretty well. Your colleagues are happy. You get several compliments. It's all good! Except for some reason, you keep obsessing about *that one thing* you did wrong—that moment when you realized that two of your PowerPoint slides were in the wrong order and one had a typo, too. You keep replaying *that one thing* inside your mind. It's almost like all of the positive moments don't count. It's the negative ones that you remember most vividly! Ugh, why?

For a whole variety of reasons, most people tend to be pretty hard on themselves. We tend to obsess over our mistakes instead of celebrating our wins. We beat ourselves up rather than cheering ourselves on. Whether it's a presentation or a first date or looking at your body in the mirror, we tend to hyper-focus on what's "not great" or how we've "messed up."

Enough, I say! It's time for you to become a cheerleader for yourself instead of a bully. It's time for you to say to yourself, "You know what? I'm doing pretty darn great."

There's no need to wait for other people to acknowledge your greatness. You can satisfy that longing by giving yourself the kudos you deserve.

When you look in the mirror, say, "Looking good, superstar."

When you arrive on time for a meeting, *give yourself the proverbial pat on the back.*

When you get enough sleep, *congratulate yourself for not watching that next episode on Netflix.*

You're doing great. You really are. Today, take some time to appreciate all the ways you are rocking this thing called life.

The more you appreciate everything that's going awesomely in your life, the more energized and optimistic you'll feel...and the faster you'll make your wish come true!

WITNESS: Today, see if you can catch yourself silently criticizing yourself for something you did or said. Catch it in the moment and see if you can say "I'm doing great!" instead.

WRITE: What's something you constantly say to yourself that no longer serves you? What can you say to yourself instead to remind yourself of how awesome you really are?

DAY 14: REMEMBER WHY YOU STARTED

You've got a wish. Obviously, you want your wish to come true. But *why*?

What's the reason this feels so important?

Once your wish comes true, how will your life change?

How will you feel when it comes true?

How will your wish coming true impact others?

Basically, do you understand *why* you want this particular wish to come true? If not, see if you can do some exploring and figure that out. Once you understand why you've got this particular wish, it becomes much easier to stay motivated and keep working steadily toward your goal.

I have days in my business when I find myself groaning over Excel spreadsheets, questioning my next move, or wondering what I need to delegate. When I'm having one of those days, I remind myself *why* I'm bothering with all of this hard work.

Why should I finish editing this boring Excel spreadsheet? Because I love being self-employed. Because I love creating products and making things that inspire people. Because I want to touch people's lives. That's why.

Once I've reconnected with all the reasons why I want to run a business, then I feel re-energized and ready to tackle the task at hand!

On tough days, I also turn toward my favorite music, books, and podcasts for an extra kick of motivation. One of my favorite podcasts is *How I Built This*. Every episode features heroic tales of entrepreneurs who had a vision and made it happen. They dug deep, figured it out as they went along, and stayed connected to their vision of *why* they wanted it in the first place.

Seeing your wish—*really seeing it and feeling it as if it's already come true*—is the first step on this journey. Next, you've got to keep taking action, day after day, to bring that wish into reality. When your energy starts to falter, when you feel like giving up, remind yourself *why* you're doing this. *Why* you started this. *Why* it's worth it to finish this journey, too.

Here you are, two weeks into making your wish come true. You've already put in lots of energy and effort. Why is it important to *you* to keep going?

Once you know the answer to that question, you'll never give up trying...until your wish becomes your reality.

WITNESS: Today, ask someone: "Why?" Why did they choose their school? Why did they pick that outfit? Why do they listen to that podcast? It's fascinating to discover why people feel called to do what they do.

WRITE: Think about your number one wish. Why does this particular wish speak to you? Why are you willing to work so hard to pursue it?

DAY 15: BREATHE

It's always go, go, go, right? From the moment we open our eyes, our bodies seem to be in perpetual motion. The other day I caught myself holding my breath. No, I wasn't underwater. I was reading the news on my phone. Yikes.

When I suddenly realized what I was doing (since I really did need to breathe after all), I looked up, dropped my jaw and allowed fresh air to drop into my belly. You know what? I instantly felt better—despite the shocking news of the day.

When you take a couple of big, deep breaths, you activate the parasympathetic nervous system (PNS) which triggers your body to relax. It's pretty amazing when you think about. Just by taking a few deep breaths, you're actually changing what's happening inside your body—almost like you're taking medication, except it's all natural and free, with no side effects! By choosing to take deep, mindful breaths, you are shifting your body's energy to slow down and get focused.

Try it for yourself. Get comfortable, close your eyes, and release any tension that you are aware of in your body. Place your right hand on your lower belly, just below your navel. Place your left hand on your upper chest. As you breathe IN through your nose, gently send the air to your right hand, just over your lower belly. As you breathe OUT through your mouth, feel the air release from the bottom of your belly up through your upper chest.

IN – Your breath fills your belly.

OUT – Your breath moves up from your belly and out your mouth.

Repeat for a minute or so. Notice if you feel any shifts in your body.

Wishwork is about playing with new ways of seeing the world and experiencing it firsthand. Today, start with your breath.

WITNESS: Find one moment today where you catch yourself holding your breath—or taking short, shallow little breaths—because you're caught up in the hectic pace of life. Pause and take three deep breaths.

WRITE: Reflect on those moments in life that make you anxious. Write down how those moments might be different if you decided to stop and take three deep breaths. When you are calm, you see all of life's possibilities.

DAY 16: FLIP THE SWITCH

Life is filled with tiny things that can drain our energy and take us out of our groove. Annoying customer service phone calls. Traffic for miles. A stain on your favorite shirt. Or your dang missing keys! Whatever the case may be, if you're allowing yourself to get annoyed, then you're zapping yourself of precious energy.

Being annoyed is simply a state of mind—and one that's not particularly fun. The good news is, you can change your mindset from *annoyed* to something else—*curious, optimistic, grateful, hopeful*—in just seconds. It's like flipping a light switch. Click! You simply decide to look at things differently.

Tons of traffic? You could allow yourself to get annoyed, drained, zapped. Or you could say, "Awesome! Now I have time to listen to India.Arie's latest album from start to finish!"

Need to make a big quarterly tax payment? That means it's been a great year in business for you!

You're all out of coffee and milk...again?! Great excuse to pop outside and get some fresh air on your way to the store.

Today, when you encounter one of life's inevitable speed bumps, see if you can immediately shift your attitude from annoyed to something more positive. Notice how this changes your energy levels. If you keep switching yourself into that positive mindset, I am willing to bet you'll feel a lot less zapped at the end of the day.

WITNESS: Notice when you are feeling drained or irritated today. What exactly is zapping your energy? Is there a different, more positive way to look at this situation?

WRITE: What's one tiny thing you can stop doing that will help you get closer to your wish?

DAY 17: GET THE SCOOP

Information is power. You may not know specifically how to fulfill your wish, but perhaps you can get a little closer if you just do a wee bit of research.

Not sure where to begin? Start by visualizing your wish. When you visualize living inside of your wish, and having it come true, do you see any specific details? A particular location? A distinctive paint color on the walls? These tiny revelations are insights from the deepest part of your being about what you're ready to allow into your life. This vision is filled with clues.

If you haven't visualized your wish coming true yet—or if it's been awhile and you don't remember the details clearly—try it again right now.

Close your eyes, breathe deeply for a few moments, and then imagine a white light pouring out of your heart. Imagine this white light turning into a projector screen—the kind of screen that movies play on. Visualize your greatest wish appearing on this screen, playing out just like a scene in a movie. It's happening. It's fulfilled. Your wish is complete and you're right there, seeing it and experiencing it.

What do you see on the screen? Is it morning or night? Is it chilly or warm? What are you wearing? Who is with you? Where are you? Is there anything specific that you notice in the environment or the room? Try to see and feel as many details as you can.

While leading a Wishbeads workshop, one of the women who attended shared a frustrating dilemma with me. She'd been struggling to refinance her home for over a year, but kept running into various roadblocks with the bank. The process had become so stressful and burdensome. When she did the visualization exercise that I just described, suddenly, she saw...her new home. It was a modern, two-story home that had a beautiful abstract painting over the fireplace.

She opened her eyes from the visualization and was gobsmacked. For an entire year, she had been trying, trying, trying *so hard* to get her house refinanced—and somehow, in the midst of all that stress, it never occurred to her, "I could just sell my current house and move somewhere new!" After doing the visualization, she felt clear and excited. Shortly after that workshop, she called a broker and started looking at modern homes (with fireplaces, of course!).

Another woman shared that, during her visualization, she saw a large table filled with her friends and family. There was loads of delicious Italian food and everyone was having the best time, laughing and sharing the meal together. She went home and started researching delicious Italian recipes to prepare.

She didn't know why her heart was craving a big, lively dinner party, but once she saw it inside her mind, she knew, "This is something I want to create."

Your wish is just waiting to come to life. With a little curiosity and a dash of effort, you can make your wish a reality. Start by visualizing your wish and searching for clues. Just like a detective or a journalist, dive into the story and get the scoop.

WITNESS: Making your wish come true takes desire, clarity, drive, and often, a bit of research. When it comes to making your wish come true, what's one thing you need to find, solve, or figure out? Set a timer for ten minutes and do some research. Notice how it feels to research and get a little closer to the answers you need. (Do you feel excited? Curious? Optimistic? Motivated to keep working?).

WRITE: What's one thing you could borrow, rent, buy, or do right now that will help you get closer to your wish? How could you gather the info that you need? For starters, why not simply Google "How to _____"?

DAY 18: GO FOR IT

Be bold enough to use your voice, brave enough to listen to your heart, and strong enough to live the life you have always imagined.

—Anonymous

Today let's kick things up a notch, shall we? Today I invite you to take a bold step toward your wish. Baby steps are awesome but today, don't take a baby step. Today, take a big step. Today, really, seriously *go for it*.

Ask yourself, *What is my wish? What's something specific that I can do, today, to move boldly in the direction of having what I desire?*

Is your wish to stand in front of an audience, rocking your TED talk? *Then apply online to speak at your local TEDx event and see if you can get booked as a speaker. (It might not even be as hard as you think!)*

Is your wish to own a new home overlooking an expansive garden? *Then head out to some open houses and meet a new real estate agent.*

Is your wish to crush the Spartan Race with effortless ease? *Then find the nearest gym and sign up for a membership.*

It's wonderful to visualize your wish, to write about your wish, and take tiny steps toward your wish. But today, I'm inviting you to take a much bigger step. Potentially, a much scarier step. Yes, this might require an extra burst of bravery. Sure, you may feel a little hesitant. Yep, I can imagine a part of you might even feel foolish. Feel all those feelings and take action anyway!

Making your wish come true requires a wee bit of hustle and a dash of "*Why not?!*"

Today, GO BIG. See where your bravery takes you.

> **WITNESS:** Today, challenge yourself to step outside your comfort zone. Do something that feels big, exciting, and even a little scary. Notice the rush of confidence (and pride!) that you feel once you've DONE THE THING.
>
> **WRITE:** What is one thing that freaks you out a little bit—something you know you need to do in order to make your wish come true? Write down what it is *and* when you are going to do it. The sooner, the better!

DAY 19: FAST FORWARD

Imagine two people who share the exact same wish: to earn five thousand dollars and then use that money for a luxurious trip to Europe.

Person #1 is hungry to make this wish come true. She's focused. She's also stressed, frustrated, and wants things to move along faster. She walks around with her eyebrows furrowed, a grimace on her face, staring down at her phone and obsessively checking her email to see if any new client bookings have come in. At the end of each day, she sighs heavily and berates herself for not getting "more" done. Her attitude is, "Why is this so *hard* and why is everything taking so *long*?"

Person #2 is equally hungry to make this wish come true. She's focused. She's also excited, thrilled, and filled with optimism. In a way, she already feels as if her wish has come true! She walks around with a smile on her face, greeting people with joy, navigating the world with enthusiasm and gratitude. She keeps her eyes wide open—noticing, witnessing, searching for clues that might guide her closer to her goal. Her attitude is, "My wish is unfolding. It's all coming true. I just need to keep working steadily and soon, I'll be there!"

Two people. Same goal. Different attitudes. Which person is going to make her wish come true faster and with greater ease? I absolutely bet…Person #2.

In fact, I bet Person #2 will achieve her wish *plus* some extra rewards, too. She'll get upgraded into a fancy hotel suite (because she's so darn delightful and the hotel concierge loves her spirit) and she'll make new friends in Italy (they fall in love with her immediately, too), and next summer, she'll be invited to housesit at their villa and she'll get a second European vacation—for free!

When you move through the world filled with excitement and gratitude, sending love outward, your wish feels the love...and your wish comes just a bit closer to you.

Close your eyes. Fast forward in time. See yourself living your wish. Feel the emotions that you experience in that time and place—the joy, pride, confidence, exhilaration, serenity, whatever you feel. Really be there. Allow the moment to unfold.

Now, imagine if you walked around today feeling those feelings *as if your wish had already come true.*

How would that shift your day?

How would that affect your energy?

How would that change your interactions with people?

The Law of Attraction states that what we focus on, we attract. When we hold those good thoughts and feelings—the sheer delight that our wish has come true—that energy attracts similar energy.

Opportunities pop up out of nowhere. A simple smile leads to a meaningful conversation. Resistance gives way to ease.

When we allow our minds to fast forward into our future desired state of being, we choose to bring that energy to the present moment. By doing this, you're bringing yourself closer to your wish—and bringing your wish closer to you. You're closing the gap between where you are and where you'd like to be.

WITNESS: Take a moment today and think about how you created the life you are living right now. Look around and see the people near you. Touch the objects in your home. Hear the sounds of life outside your window.

WRITE: How will you feel when your wish comes true? What will your day-to-day life look like when it comes true? How will your life be different than it is now? Write it all down.

DAY 20: GO WITH THE FLOW

You've probably experienced that beautiful mental state called "the flow."

It's a state when you're fully immersed in the task at hand, totally engaged, and your actions and ideas flow along with ease.

Maybe you're planting baby tomatoes in your garden, fully immersed, and you spend two hours and barely even notice the time passing. Or you lose track of time as you dig into a puzzle. Or you peacefully zone out while balancing your checkbook to the penny. Or you start powering through your inbox, rapidly answering emails, and suddenly (whoa!) it's down to zero.

There are certain activities that invite our minds to get quiet and "get into the flow." For me, it's organizing a closet. All the clearing, sorting, and cleaning helps me relax. Inevitably, once the task is complete, I find that my mind is equally cleared.

When I'm having one of those days where I feel zapped or stuck, I find a space to tidy. It can be a drawer, my desk, or even the fridge. Once I finish up—BOOM—I inevitably find myself with more energy and clarity so that I can move forward. When my space is clean, my mind is clear.

I now use this insight as a tool. If I'm feeling overwhelmed with all the details of running a household, juggling the kids' schedules, running my business, and having a healthy social life, I know it's time to devote a Sunday to cleaning out the garage! That always helps me to get back into the flow.

So, what types of activities get *you* into the flow?

When do you find yourself lost in a task? What are the moments when the inner chatter stops and you are not even aware of the passing time? What hobbies give you energy? What gets your brain into that wonderful flow-state? Maybe (like me) it's tidying. Or maybe it's walking, meditating, cooking, braiding your kid's hair, folding laundry, writing "thank you" notes to friends, some other activity.

When you find what works for you, you have a tool to help you tap into your personal power. By quieting your mind, you are allowing a part of yourself to transcend to a greater plane of awareness where you gain insights and energy that you can bring back into your everyday life.

As you work toward your wish, try to get yourself into the flow-state as often as possible. See what happens when you go with the flow. You will accomplish more with less effort. See for yourself!

WITNESS: Notice a moment today when you are totally at ease doing something that comes naturally to you.

WRITE: Think about your skills and talents. What comes easily to you? Writing? Connecting with people? Planning? Organizing? Tidying? How can you use the skills you already have to make your wish come true?

DAY 21: TRUST

Wow. You did it. For three weeks, you gave yourself the gift of focusing on your wish. You took action toward your dream and made a series of tiny steps, had small (or big!) discoveries, while taking big leaps of faith.

What's been happening for you? Are you closer to your wish? Are you feeling optimistic and excited? Have serendipitous things been happening for you lately? If you have stories to share, please do! Just send me a note at hello@wishbeads.com.

Over the last twenty-one days, I invited you to do a little writing at the end of each day. Perhaps you wrote things down inside a journal, on your computer, or scribbled in this book! Wherever you wrote, I hope you'll hold onto these writings as a beautiful record of this Wishwork experience.

I encourage you to go back and read what you wrote down again... and again! When you're having one those days when you feel zapped or uninspired, go back and read to remind yourself of what you can achieve when you put your attention and effort toward what you wish to manifest.

There is power in those pages. Use them anytime you want to tap back into their strength.

Learning to trust yourself is a process unto itself, so be patient as you develop this ability. These twenty-one days of Wishwork are here for you whenever you need them. You can repeat this twenty-one-day process anytime...and you can focus on a new wish every time!

If your wish didn't come true in the last three weeks, be patient. Step back and consider the positive shifts that did occur. What happened that gave you evidence that your efforts paid off? Are you happier? More content? Excited about the future? Fired up to wish for bigger and brighter dreams? Keep up the great work! If your wish did come true, then by all means, wish again!

There is no genie offering you a limited number of wishes. Your ability to wish is endless.

When you wake up feeling a bit more positive and hopeful, you brighten the lives of everyone around you. Fulfilling your wishes is truly an act of selfless giving. When you win, everyone wins, too.

The more wishes that come true, the happier this world will be.

Thank you for trusting the process. Thank you for trusting yourself. Thank you for being *you*. Shine on.

WITNESS: Trust that you have all you need to make your wish come true. For twenty-one days in a row, you showed up. You did the work. You gave yourself the gift of wishing. Today, keep your eyes open. Look for a sign that all is well and that you're on your way to achieving all you desire.

WRITE: It's time to take note of all you have accomplished in the last twenty-one days. How do you feel? What signs did you receive? What surprises did you have? What lessons were learned? What part of your wish has already come true? Take a moment and jot all of this down now. See how far you have come!

Watch It Come True

BE "THERE" ALREADY

Close your eyes for a moment and picture your greatest wish, once again. Really use your imagination to be there right now. What are you wearing? What do you hear? What tiny details catch your eye? How do you feel? Soak in as many details as possible.

Isn't it fun to mentally transport yourself—to be right where you wish to be? Can you feel the shift in your energy? Does the world seem a bit different than it was a moment ago?

Every time you connect to your wish, you are planting magical seeds of what you wish to manifest.

Think about it: a seed contains everything it needs to reach its full potential. One little seed grows to become a fruit to feed the hungry. One little seed can become a flower that provides nectar to butterflies and bees. One little seed can become an enormous Redwood tree that can live for one thousand years!

But seeds need nourishment to grow.

When you do your daily Wishwork, you are feeding the seed of your wish, giving it valuable energy and attention so it can grow and flourish. When you stay positive and proactive, you are living your wish, as if it has already come true!

That's what it means to "be there already." Despite your current circumstances, you are choosing to feel the feelings you would experience as if your wish has already come true.

But, wait, Alexa! You mean I am supposed to pretend that my wish already came true?

Yep. That's what I'm saying.

Instead of panicking every time you see your pile of bills—pause, breathe, and see yourself living the abundant life you deserve. Feed that seed with your energy and attention.

Yes, you will still need to pay your bills, but when you can calm yourself down, you are able to think more clearly and creatively, which will inevitably help you prosper. If you beat yourself down with the same old negative self-talk—*I'm horrible with money, I'll never get ahead*—you are zapping your energy and sabotaging your success.

As I mentioned earlier, what you focus on, you attract.

By connecting to your wish regularly and imagining that your wish has already come true, you are feeding the seed of your desires—nurturing them until they grow, pierce the surface, and become visible.

Celebrate Every Win

Most people wait until something "huge" and "amazing" happens before they allow themselves to celebrate. Maybe you're thinking, *Once my wish comes true, then I'll throw a party! I'll get a cake! I'll tell all my friends! Oh man, that day is going to be incredible! A major celebration!* Yes, you should absolutely celebrate when your wish comes true. But why wait until then? Why not celebrate every little victory along the way to getting there, every green light, every achievement, every single one? Wouldn't that make life a whole lot more fun?

From the moment I launched Wishbeads, I saw the potential for all it could be, but I was also well aware of the epic amount of hustle it was going to take to get there. I asked everyone I knew for advice and introductions. Deep down, I trusted that this vision of mine would unfold just as it was meant to, but it would be up to me to stay positive. For every yes, there were always a few nos. For every big break, I certainly had some closed doors. When things appeared to not go as well as I hoped, I would look for signs that all was well.

Which brings me back to Oprah...

I had the good fortune to be introduced to the editor of Oprah.com through a very dear friend of mine. I scheduled a meeting during one of my trips to New York and, as I checked into security at the Conde Nast Building, I had to pinch myself that I was heading up to the Oprah offices.

The meeting went well. I showed my friend's friend—and a few other fine folks—my Wishbeads paper bead kit and everyone seemed to like it. There were no fireworks or anyone jumping on the phone to call Ms. Winfrey, but I was tickled to be there. As I was heading back down the elevator, I wasn't quite ready to hit the streets of Manhattan just yet. I still wanted to soak it all in.

As luck would have it, the elevator opened up on the mezzanine floor where there was a lovely cafeteria. I decided that a quick bite might be the perfect ending to this highlight of my trip. Gathering a beverage and a rice bowl, I headed to the cashier and when she told me the total, I just about fell over.

$11.11

The number 11:11 is considered to be a lucky set of numbers—like a little wink from the Universe letting you know that you're on the right track. I'm one of those people who sees 11:11 every day. Usually twice a day! It's a rather strange phenomenon that many others experience. There are even books written about it. For me, every time I catch the clock at that time, I feel like I'm getting a virtual high five.

Standing in line to pay, I will confess that a tiny part of me questioned if the meeting went as well as it could. Some sneaky thoughts popped in.

Did I say the right thing? Did they get my big vision? Did they think Oprah would think this is so cool that she'll want to hang out with me and do a Super Soul session chat under those lovely trees in Santa Barbara?! Or maybe the meeting wasn't that great?

Lots of doubts circled in my mind. But then when the cashier handed me my receipt, I felt like it was a win! A sign that all is well. A message for me to keep going! Trust the path! Stay positive! I enjoyed my rice bowl and it felt like a celebration. Even though Oprah's team didn't offer me a two-page feature in the magazine right on the spot, just being at Oprah HQ felt like a "win."

As you do the Wishwork, look for reasons to celebrate. A surprise five-dollar bill in your coat pocket. A friend who makes a helpful introduction. That moment when the clock strikes 11:11. Getting your very first piece of writing published somewhere, even if it doesn't pay anything...yet! Reasons to celebrate are everywhere. No matter how small they are, celebrate each and every win. This makes life more fun (and makes you a more pleasant person to be around), it pumps up your energy levels, and it makes every single day of your journey feel like a victory.

Common Questions

As you do the work—and watch your wish begin to come true—
inevitably, some questions will arise in your mind!

Here are a few that I've heard and my best advice for navigating
the wonderful world of wishing. Of course, you are welcome to
hear real stories that we highlight on the Wishbeads blog, our
podcast *Wishbeads*, and on Instagram @wishbeads.official. Meet
your fellow Wishcrafters! They're pretty awesome people...

**What if I have a beautiful wish that's clear and specific, but it
involves my spouse, and he/she doesn't share the same wish?
(For example: I'm wishing for a modern two-story home with a
fireplace but my husband doesn't want to move.)**

> This can be tricky! Of course life involves others,
> especially when it's around big decisions like moving
> into a new home. I would encourage you to go deeper
> within this vision and ask yourself how you can bring
> more of this experience into your current life without
> needing cooperation from anyone. Where can you take
> full responsibility for bringing this modern feel into your
> present situation? For example, when I'm standing in
> a modern home, I love the sparseness and clean lines.
> If I walked into my current home—more of a beachy
> bungalow—I may head over to my desk area to see what
> items I can part with so I can sit down to a clean, spare
> desk when I sit down to work. On a Sunday morning,
> when I'm leafing through the pages of *Dwell* magazine,
> I may cut out images that inspire me and heck, I may
> even share them with my hubby as we think about our
> future pad. It's a more gentle approach that allows you

to find joy in the small shifts while planting seeds for the future manifestation.

What if my wish is really, really big? How can I stay motivated to keep working for years, even decades, to make it come true?

Ah, here is where I encourage you to not be attached to the timeline. In my own career, I was an actress for a decade before I began creating online courses and teaching individuals and corporations how to speak with confidence and ignite their 1,000-watt presence. Then, after doing that for years, the idea for Wishbeads came to me. While those stages in my life seem very different, they are really stepping stones for where I am today—each phase teaching me something so invaluable, the knowledge of which I used to grow into my next business. No experience is ever wasted. None. When you can learn to trust the journey, you become less attached to the final outcome. Staying motivated simply means that you keep doing the Wishwork and you never give up. Your personal experiences doing the Wishwork will inspire you along the way and very well may lead to the big, glorious wish you wanted in the first place.

What if my wish depends on someone else "offering" something to me? For example, what if I'm wishing for a book deal with Random House, or an Academy Award, or a marriage proposal? I can't control other people and "make" them do things, nor would I want to, so is this a foolish type of wish?

No, it's not foolish in the least! Wishing is more fun when you push yourself to move into the direction of your best and boldest life. Sure, those examples you mentioned all involve many people saying YES to what you want, but all of those scenarios require you to take action above all else. Random House can't say yes to a book you never wrote. Steven Spielberg can't hire you for his movie if you never audition. Your future husband can't get down on one knee if you never bothered to give Match.com a try. Everything starts with you. Trust that and enjoy the journey of doing. You'll never regret trying!

I've tried doing the visualization that you suggested. But for some reason I can't "see" my wish clearly. I don't know what I want, or what's going to make me feel fulfilled. Help please!

If the vision of your wish isn't coming to you right away, then keep asking, *What is my wish?* Gently allow yourself to stay with this question, with an attitude of curiosity and compassion. When you wake up in the morning and before you go to sleep, repeat this statement, "Thank you for showing me what will make me happy. Thank you for revealing my wish." When you ask, you are more likely to receive.

I have so many wishes that I want, can't I just wish for them all at once?

Oh, it's so tempting to write a monster list of wishes, make oodles of Wishbeads bracelets, and wish for them all at once! If you're doing the Wishwork for the first time, however, my suggestion is to trust the experience and focus on one wish. When you do, you'll see how the connections, coincidences, and your actions add up. You'll see the power you have to make specific shifts in your life and the impact they have on how you feel and what people and opportunities are attracted to you. By sticking with a specific wish, you'll be able to see how the Wishwork truly works. The good news is that there is no limit to what you can wish for, so feel free to wish as many times as you want! (No genie required.)

I have someone in my life that is really struggling and I want to wish for them. Do you suggest doing the Wishwork for someone other than yourself?

I really do believe in the power of prayer and when people in my life are going through tough challenges; I envision them being healthy, healed, and happy. I hold onto that vision, or wish, in my heart, and in some cases I even create a Wishbeads bracelet with that wish inside. When it comes to the Wishwork journey, however, that is all about my heart's desire. My wish. My future. My happiness and fulfillment. Why? Because you are the only person responsible for making your wish come true. Not your parents. Not your government. Not your boss. It takes work and with the right guidance and attitude, you'll be supported in ways that you cannot anticipate. That's what the Wishwork is all about... See for yourself.

Do you have a question that you would love for me to answer? Just send me a note to hello@wishbeads.com. I'd be happy to answer your questions on my blog, on a podcast episode, or even in a future revised edition of this book. Thanks for asking!

Final Thoughts

MY BIG WISH

On Day 12 of the Wishwork process, you are invited to say your wish out loud. There's something about giving it voice that sets change in motion. I mean, how can people help you if they don't know what you want in the first place?

So, here it is. My big, glorious wish and I'm honored to share it with you.

One million people wishing at once.

One million people coming together at a single moment in time to see what's possible.

One million people committed to making their wishes come true.

When this many people come together with this singular intention, we can bring a very special energy to this planet. We can bring hope, connection, positivity and kindness to the world. And this individual happiness can spread its wings and touch others you come into contact with. A ripple effect of goodness.

Instead of feeling powerless in the face of bickering world leaders, dramatic climate change, and day-to-day hostility, you can claim your own joy. You came into this world for a reason. Maybe it's simply to make your own wishes come true.

When you take action, you change your life. When one million people take action, you change the world.

With Deep Gratitude

There are some very special people who have made my wishes come true along the way and I am so humbled and honored for their support, love, and encouragement. Thank you to my spiritual teacher, whom I've meditated with for the past sixteen years, and our incredible group of students. The light of teaching is inside every aspect of this book and every Wishbeads experience. May it continue to shine.

To my friends and fellow entrepreneurs who have guided me with their wisdom, their experience, their connections, and introductions. Your generosity knows no bounds! All of the late night calls, showing up and helping me pack Wishbeads kits, pouring over my QuickBooks, connecting me to the greatest manufacturer, high fiving the big breaks, and offering hugs during the small setbacks. I've learned so much from you all and there is no way I could have created this without your help!

A special thanks to my writing teacher, Alexandra Franzen, who has an innate ability to sneak inside your psyche and pull out just what you want to say in the clearest way possible—I thank you for guiding me throughout the creation of this book. Your deep, compassionate soul is embedded in every one of these pages.

Lastly, to my amazing family for always supporting my wishes in whatever form they take. You are my heart and soul. I love you so.

Keep Wishing!

You've reached the end of this book. Keep wishing, keep working to make your wishes come true, and keep the momentum going!

You can order a Wishbeads bracelet at Wishbeads.com. These bracelets make a beautiful gift for yourself, a friend, a bridal shower, baby shower, wedding, anniversary, birthday, New Year's Day brunch—any kind of occasion where people are making new wishes or embarking on a new adventure.

You can download the free Wishbeads app at:
https://www.wishbeads.com/yes

You can listen to inspiring stories on our Podcast at:
https://www.wishbeads.com/podcast

You can hire the author of this book (yes, that's me!) to lead a Wishcircle workshop at your next conference, festival, or at your company, or to give a keynote talk on how to create a positive and proactive mindset, how to build motivation, and how to stay focused and make big things happen. More info on that, here:
https://www.wishbeads.com/events.

You can post a photo of your wish-in-progress using the #Wishwork hashtag. Go ahead and post a photo of your to-do list (with tons of items checked off—hooray for progress!), your art studio (with a painting halfway done!), your pile of sweaty gym clothes (proof that you're working hard on your goals!) or some other snapshot of your life. Take a photo to show the world, "I am doing the work to make my wishes come true."

Have something you'd like to share? Your next big wish? An exciting victory? Maybe you tried something that was suggested in this book and it worked out victoriously? Send a note to hello@wishbeads.com and share away.

Thank you for reading this book.

May all of your wishes come true.

ABOUT THE AUTHOR

Alexa Fischer is the founder of Wishbeads, a company with a mission to inspire millions of people to make exciting wishes, take action, put in the work, and make those wishes come true.

In addition to running Wishbeads, she also works as a TV/film actor and public speaking coach. She lives in Santa Monica, CA, with her husband, two kids, a white fluffy rescue dog, and a bright red 1961 Shasta Airflyte trailer which serves as her outdoor office. You can find Alexa's creations at Wishbeads.com and the rest of her work at AlexaFischer.com.

the tiny press

At The Tiny Press, we believe that small actions—and small books—can create a big ripple effect in our world.

Our mission is to create short books around 100 pages that are inspiring, uplifting, and encouraging.

We know you have lots of priorities in your life—work, family, errands, and more. Sometimes it can feel like there's "just no time left" to curl up with a book. We hope Tiny Press can provide a happy solution by offering short, "tiny" books—books that make sense for busy people with full, demanding lives.

With each book, our goal is to make your day a little better than it was before.

Founded in 2018 by Alexandra Franzen (alexandrafranzen.com) in collaboration with Mango Publishing (mango.bz).

Find more Tiny Press books on the Mango website, on Amazon, and everywhere books are sold.